W9-AAE-034

BLUE BANNER
BIOGRAPHY

Tim
TEBOW

Fox River Valley PLD
555 Barrington Ave.
Dundee, IL 60118
www.frvpld.info Renew online or call 847-590-8706

John A. Torres

Mitchell Lane
PUBLISHERS
P.O. Box 196
Hockessin, Delaware 19707
Visit us on the web: www.mitchelllane.com
Comments? Email us: mitchelllane@mitchelllane.com

Mitchell Lane
PUBLISHERS

Printing   1   2   3   4   5   6   7   8   9

Blue Banner Biographies

Library of Congress Cataloging-in-Publication Data applied for.
Torres, John Albert.
 Tim Tebow / by John Torres.
  p. cm. — (Blue banner biographies)
 Includes bibliographical references and index.
 ISBN 978-1-61228-317-3 (library bound)
 1. Tebow, Tim, 1987– —Juvenile literature. 2. Football players—United States—Biography—Juvenile literature. 3. Quarterbacks (Football)—United States—Biography—Juvenile literature. I. Title.
 GV939.T423T67 2013
 796.332092—dc23
 [B]
                                                                                          2012018313
eBook ISBN: 9781612283883

ABOUT THE AUTHOR: John A. Torres is a sports columnist for *Florida Today* newspaper. He has covered many sporting events, including Tim Tebow's first start of the 2011 season against the Miami Dolphins. Torres was part of the press corps that interviewed Tebow after the game. Torres is a published author with more than 50 books to his credit. Learn more about him on www.johnatorres. com and follow him @johnalbertorres on Twitter.

PUBLISHER'S NOTE: The following story has been thoroughly researched, and to the best of our knowledge represents a true story. While every possible effort has been made to ensure accuracy, the publisher will not assume liability for damages caused by inaccuracies in the data and makes no warranty on the accuracy of the information contained herein. This story has not been authorized or endorsed by Tim Tebow.

Blue Banner Biography

When Tim Tebow was drafted by the Denver Broncos, experts criticized his passing style and wondered whether he could achieve the same success in the NFL that he had enjoyed in college.

Hero

*I*t had already been a game for the ages. No one had expected the Denver Broncos to make the playoffs and yet here they were, going toe-to-toe with the defending AFC champions, the rough and ready Pittsburgh Steelers.

The once-proud Broncos franchise had not made the playoffs in six seasons and had not won a Super Bowl since 1999.

The city of Denver, nicknamed the "Mile-High City," seemed to be just that. Fans were as excited about the Broncos' return to the playoffs as they were the hard-to-define quarterback — sometimes playing more like a fullback — who led them there: Tim Tebow.

Tebow had revolutionized the offense and was sometimes gaining more yards on the ground running with the ball than he was passing it. When he did drop back to pass it was often ugly, as he missed open receivers and had an awkward throwing motion unlike any quarterback in the National Football League. But there was something about this second-year player from the University of Florida that simply electrified fans and teammates alike: he was a winner.

He had a knack for playing poorly for most of the game, only to come alive in the fourth quarter and lead the Broncos to one improbable victory after another. Tebow had commandeered the offense to overtime victories against the Miami Dolphins, San Diego Chargers, and Chicago Bears.

They also defeated the New York Jets when Tebow scrambled into the end zone from 20 yards out as the final seconds ticked away.

Just the fact that the Broncos had made the post-season was reason enough for fans to celebrate. No one gave them much of a chance to beat the team from Pittsburgh, known for its bruising defense and style of play.

But now, here were the Broncos and the Steelers, duking it out on the field on a chilly January afternoon in Denver. The score was tied, 23-23 and the Broncos would be getting the ball first in the overtime period. If Tebow was somehow able to lead his team on a touchdown scoring drive, then the contest would be over.

> *Tebow had revolutionized the offense and was sometimes gaining more yards on the ground running with the ball than he was passing it.*

The stadium was literally shaking as fans jumped up and down, anticipating victory. The roar was deafening, and television announcers practically had to yell into their microphones to be heard.

The Broncos took over on their own 20-yard line.

What happened next was simply electric, even to someone who's not the world's biggest football fan.

For most of the game, Tebow had utilized the wishbone option offense, something used mainly in high school and colleges. This kind of offense usually involves the quarterback taking off and running on his own. On several plays throughout the game, Tebow had done just that.

So the Steelers had started sending their two safeties — defensive backs that are the last defense against a long pass — close to the line of scrimmage to help stop Tebow and the Denver running attack. Now, with the game on the line, offensive coordinator Mike McCoy expected them to do this again, so he called another type of play.

Tebow led the team out of the huddle, barked some signals and received the snapped football from his center. And just as McCoy had thought, the Steelers were sending their safeties on a blitz. Tebow's eyes widened as he saw his wide receiver Demaryius Thomas cut across the middle of the field. He was wide open with just a cornerback trailing him. Tebow knew that if he got his teammate the ball with a perfect pass in stride, then it would be a footrace to the end zone.

There was neither hesitation nor ugliness in this pass. Tebow delivered the ball in picture-perfect fashion and Thomas caught the 18-yard pass in stride. Then, like a racehorse, he galloped the final 62 yards to the end zone as the Broncos fans erupted with glee.

After completing an 80-yard touchdown pass to wide receiver Demaryius Thomas, Tebow kneels to thank God. That pass resulted in an overtime win for the Broncos against the Pittsburgh Steelers. Tebow is known for speaking openly about his Christian faith.

The upstart Denver Broncos had defeated the mighty Steelers 29-23 to eliminate Pittsburgh from the playoffs.

Tebow dropped to a knee and thanked God, an action which had become famous as "Tebowing."

Then he ran around the stadium, slapping hands with fans in the stands.

Tim Tebow had gone from benchwarmer to playoff-winning quarterback in one season. But it didn't happen without hard work — Tim Tebow is a person who thrives under pressure and never folds in the face of adversity.

Growing Up

*T*imothy Richard Tebow was born on August 14, 1987 in the unlikeliest of places for a future NFL quarterback.

Tebow was born in Makati City in the country of the Philippines. Tebow's parents, Pam and Bob, were working there as Christian missionaries. But nothing seems to come easy for Tim Tebow, including being born.

While living in the Philippines, Tebow's mother had become very sick before she knew she was pregnant. She had even fallen into a coma after drinking contaminated water and becoming infected with a deadly amoeba. She was given powerful drugs to rouse her from her coma.

These drugs were very dangerous to her unborn baby. Pam told the *Gainesville Sun* that doctors told her the baby had suffered damage and that her life could be in danger if she continued with the pregnancy. Doctors advised her to terminate — or end — the pregnancy.

Instead, Pam and Bob turned to prayer.

"My husband just prayed that if the Lord would give us a son, that he would let us raise him," she told the *Gainesville Sun.*

Tim was born, and though he was thin and malnourished, he was in otherwise perfect health. Tebow is the youngest of five children. Even before Tim was born, his father was involved in sports. After graduating from college and the seminary where he became a pastor, Bob Tebow became one of the Florida representatives for the Fellowship of Christian Athletes.

Tebow was born in Makati City in the country of the Philippines. Tebow's parents, Pam and Bob, were working there as Christian missionaries.

The family moved back to Florida from the Philippines when Tim was just three years old. The Tebow family had always homeschooled their children and the youngest was no exception.

When he was about five years old, Tim told his parents that he wanted to play sports. His older brothers were very athletic and played sports too. The problem was that since the children were all homeschooled they might not be able to play high school sports.

But that changed in 1996 when a new Florida law was passed. The law allowed homeschooled students to play sports for the local high school where they lived.

The Tebow family lived in the Jacksonville area, so Tim played football for Trinity Christian Academy. He was a linebacker and tight end, but he really wanted to be a quarterback. At Nease High School, he would be able to play quarterback, but he and his family lived outside the school's boundaries. So he and his mother moved into an apartment in the Nease High School district. At Nease, he became a star quarterback.

Tebow wowed fans, coaches, and college recruiters alike with his ability to run and pass the ball, his incredible desire to win, and his toughness. Calling Tebow tough might be an understatement. In high school, he once played nearly an entire game with a broken bone in his leg.

Despite his increasing fame and success, Tebow remains humble and continues to devote time to helping people in need. He credits his parents, Pam and Bob (left), with instilling these values in him from a young age.

Tebow's performances with the Nease High School football team earned him national recognition from ESPN *and* Sports Illustrated. *College recruiters took notice, as well.*

As a junior, Tebow was named Florida's Player of the Year, an honor usually reserved for high school seniors. That title put Tebow on the radar of just about every major college football program in the country. Colleges wanted Tebow even more after they saw what he did during his senior year of high school.

In December 2005, Tebow led Nease to a State Championship. That season, he was once again named Florida's Player of the Year, and played for the U.S. Army High School All-American team. As a high school player, Tebow broke state yardage records for passing and rushing. He also scored an incredible 70 touchdowns in a single season.

Everyone noticed. Tebow was featured in *Sports Illustrated* and even on ESPN while he was still in high school.

The best high school players from around the country are selected each year to play in the U.S. Army All-American Bowl. In the 2006 game, high school senior Tebow was chosen to represent the East team.

Even with all the attention he was receiving, Tebow remained very humble. He was still being homeschooled, and his parents centered their lessons around the Christian values they believed in. So it was no surprise that Tebow credited all his success to God.

Choosing a college was not easy for Tim, even though both his parents had attended the University of Florida and had fallen in love there. A lot of schools offered him scholarships, including Alabama—which is one of Florida's biggest rivals. But in the end, Tebow chose to play for the University of Florida Gators.

CHAPTER 3

College Star

*T*im Tebow was a college freshman at the University of Florida in 2006. And even though Tebow was a highly sought-after recruit, college freshmen usually start their first seasons on the bench. Tebow was no different.

The Florida Gators already had a starting quarterback by the name of Chris Leak. But it was pretty clear right from the start that head coach Urban Meyer had special plans for Tebow. In fact, Tebow got his first chance to play in the season-opening game against Southern Mississippi. Tebow raced onto the field during a scoring drive near the goal line in the fourth quarter and promptly barreled in from the one-yard line for his first college touchdown during the 34-7 romp.

He became only the third freshman quarterback in Gator history to score a touchdown in his first game.

It was only the beginning. Coach Meyer would start using his talented freshman more and more. Tebow found playing time in special situations around the goal line. He also played in special formations, where he got to utilize his talents in running the ball and making passes while on the run.

The Gators were on fire that special season, compiling a 13-1 record including close, hard-fought wins against Tennessee and South Carolina. In a 23-10 win against Louisiana State University, Tebow threw his first touchdown pass. With each victory, the Gators moved up in the polls until they became the number one team in the country. Tim Tebow had a lot to do with the team's success.

He proved to be a dual threat as a top rusher and passer. He was ranked second on the team in rushing with 469 yards and eight touchdowns. He only attempted 33 passes during his freshman year, but threw for 358 yards and five touchdowns.

In the BCS National Championship Game that pits the two top college football teams against each other, Tebow gave an outstanding performance for Florida as they destroyed a powerful Ohio State team. He ran for a touchdown and passed for another as the Gators became national champions!

In 2007, the Gators lost a lot of players who had graduated from the 2006 team, but Tebow was now the starting quarterback.

Still, the team was ranked sixth in the country to start the season. Tebow was ready to show the world that he could be more than just a runner.

In his very first start, against Western Kentucky, he threw for 300 yards and three touchdowns, leading the Gators to an easy win. A few weeks later, the Gators put together a rare blowout against rival powerhouse Tennessee. Tebow led the offense to an amazing 554 yards. It seemed that something clicked for him that season, because he became a scoring machine.

Tebow became only the third freshman quarterback in Gator history to score a touchdown in his first game.

But what he did on November 10, 2007 at the University of South Carolina was epic. Tebow not only passed for more than 300 yards and threw two touchdown passes, but he also ran for five touchdowns in the game! Unfortunately, the team lost close matches against Auburn and Louisiana State University that year, eliminating any chances they had of becoming national champions for a second year in a row.

Tebow's incredible play all season long was noticed by everyone. He was considered by many to be the best college player in the country that year, and was awarded the prestigious Heisman Trophy. It was the first time an underclassman had ever won the award.

Expectations were high for Tim Tebow and the 2008 Florida Gators. The team was returning a lot of key players and many thought the team would once again contend for a national title. They were right. The only blemish in the

Gators' otherwise perfect season was a one-point loss to Ole Miss in September.

That loss affected Tebow deeply. He even apologized in his post-game press conference after the game.

"I'm sorry. I'm extremely sorry. We were hoping for an undefeated season. That was my goal, something Florida's never done here. But I promise you one thing: a lot of good

"Tebow was honored as the 73rd recipient of the prestigious Heisman Trophy following an outstanding 2007 season with the University of Florida Gators.

will come out of this. You have never seen any player in the entire country play as hard as I will play the rest of this season and you'll never see someone push the rest of the team as hard as I will push everybody the rest of this season, and you'll never see a team play harder than we will the rest of this season. God Bless."

Those comments became a rallying cry of sorts for the team who steamrolled the competition the rest of the year. During the Southeastern Conference (SEC) Championship Game, the Gators won against number one ranked Alabama. They won again when they faced the new number one ranked Oklahoma in the BCS National Championship Game.

Tebow's words were later immortalized on a plaque that was hung just outside the entrance of the team's football offices.

Against Oklahoma, Tebow passed for two touchdowns and more than 200 yards to give Florida its second national title in three seasons. He finished third that season in the Heisman Trophy voting.

In 2007, the Gators lost a lot of players who had graduated from the 2006 team, but Tebow was now the starting quarterback.

With his junior year success, there was talk of Tebow leaving college early to enter the NFL draft. After all, what more was there for the star quarterback to accomplish? He was a Heisman Trophy winner and had been a part of two national championship teams. But he promised everyone he would be back for one more season and one more shot at glory.

Championship Dreams

*A*s promised, Tim Tebow returned to the University of Florida for his senior season. For the second year in a row, Tebow was named captain of the football team. And there were high expectations. Florida was ranked number one in the polls even before the season started.

Led by Tebow, the Gators cruised to victories in their first four games before having to face a tough Louisiana State University team in Baton Rouge. This time, Florida was saved by their defense in a 13-3 Gators win. With an easy schedule the rest of the way, it looked as if the Gators were destined to play for another national title.

Throughout the season, Tebow would wear inspirational messages on the field. On the eye black strips that he wore under his eyes to block the glare from the lights, Tebow would notate bible verses in brightly-colored marker. There are very few athletes who are as comfortable talking about their faith as Tebow is.

Florida won all 12 of its regular season games, and the only thing standing between the team and another championship was the South East Conference (SEC) game against number two-ranked Alabama. The Alabama Crimson Tide had also won all of its 12 regular season games. The winner of this matchup would play the University of Texas Longhorns for the national championship.

On the eye black strips that he wore under his eyes to block the glare from the lights, Tebow would notate bible verses in brightly-colored marker.

Tebow gave everything he had in the game against Alabama. He threw for 247 yards and a touchdown, and was also Florida's leading rusher in the game, gaining 63 tough yards on the ground. But Florida had no answer for Alabama's star running back Mark Ingram, who rushed for more than 100 yards and scored three touchdowns. Alabama won the game 32-13, and would go on to beat Texas in the championship game.

An emotional Tebow cried after the game and during interviews on television.

"This not how I wanted to go out," he told reporters after the game during a televised press conference. But in typical Tebow fashion, he put the loss in perspective. During the game, he had worn a bracelet in honor of Taylor Haugen, a high school student who died after a football injury. Haugen had dreamed of playing for the Gators one day.

"Obviously I'm emotional, as you can see, after games, and it means a lot to me. But at the end of the day it's not what really matters," Tebow said. "It's still just a game. And that's why it's not life or death and it's not the biggest thing in the world."

A disappointed Tebow leaves the field following an interception in the fourth quater of the 2009 SEC Championship game between Florida and Alabama.

The Gators went on to appear in the Sugar Bowl against the University of Cincinnati. It would be Tebow's last game as a college player. He played the game of his life, completing 31 of 35 passes for 482 yards, and three touchdown passes. He also rushed for more than 50 yards as the Gators destroyed the Bearcats, 51-24.

Tebow is regarded by many as the greatest college player ever to play the game. But now that he was eligible for the NFL draft, there was a lot of debate as to whether he would be good in the pros. Professional football is very different from the college game. At Florida, Tebow had the option of running the ball or passing, but that is not the way most NFL teams operate. There was also a lot of question about Tebow's throwing style. Critics said he took too long to get rid of the football for the pro game and that his accuracy would be an issue.

No one was really sure where Tebow would be drafted. Some experts suggested that he would not even be a first round draft pick.

They were wrong. The Denver Broncos chose Tebow with the 25th pick of the first round.

"At Florida, I was asked to run a certain style of offense," Tebow told *The Denver Post* after he was drafted. "Now, I'm getting asked to do something different. I'm going to do everything possible to do that."

Tim is one of the best running quarterbacks in all of football.

What's Next?

*T*ebow started only a few games as a rookie for the Broncos, and then began the 2011 season as Kyle Orton's backup. But when the Broncos got off to a 1-4 start, the fans in Denver started chanting during games for the team to give Tebow a try.

What followed was a remarkable run by Tebow and the Broncos that was sometimes marked by ugly play and last-minute dramatics. In October 2011, Tebow started his first game of the season against the Miami Dolphins. He looked terrible. His passes fluttered and floated and the Broncos fell behind.

But with just a few minutes left in the game, everything started falling into place, as if by magic. Tebow led the Broncos on two scoring drives ending in touchdown passes, and then he ran in a two-point conversion to send the game into overtime. The Broncos won 18-15, and "Tebow magic" was born.

After the game, Tebow was more excited to talk about the work he does with children than his heroics on the field. At the beginning of the season, Tebow had launched the

Tebow's magical string of games with the Broncos began in October 2011 when he led a last-minute comeback against the Dolphins in Miami.

"W15H program," created to grant wishes to sick children. He told reporters after the game that the best part of his day had been meeting a sick teenager before the game.

"That's what matters most to me," he said. "Just to see that smile on that kid's face meant everything." Tebow meets a child battling a terminal illness before every game. He takes the child onto the field, gives them a jersey, signs autographs, and spends time with them.

What followed was a series of come-from-behind wins, usually fueled by a Tebow pass or run. He led the team to an 8-8 record and a playoff berth where the team defeated Pittsburgh before losing to New England.

After the season, the Broncos promised to work with Tebow. But later, the team had an opportunity to pick up

Tebow opened the first "Timmy's Playroom" at the headquarters of Dreams Come True, a Jacksonville-based nonprofit that fulfills the dreams of ill children. He poses here with Blake Torres, an 11-year-old "Dreams Come True" kid battling leukemia.

one of the greatest passers of all time, free agent quarterback Peyton Manning. Denver signed Manning and traded Tebow to the New York Jets.

This was a curious move for the Jets, because they already had a good quarterback in Mark Sanchez. Tebow would have to begin another season as a backup in the NFL, but the Jets promised to run special college-type plays to make sure he got some playing time.

The appeal of Tim Tebow is not limited to just his football skills. His character, his honesty, his humility, and his work with children make him one of the game's true role models.

In March 2012, just before being traded to the Jets, Tebow opened the first of what he promised would be many

Before the 2012 season, the Broncos traded Tebow to the Jets, who promised to utilize him as more than just a quarterback.

"Timmy's Playrooms." This playroom, designed to look like an NFL locker room, was made for children battling terminal diseases. This first room was located at the headquarters for Dreams Come True, a charity based in Jacksonville, Florida. More rooms would be built in hospitals around the country, Tebow said.

One of the most impressive things about Tebow is that he didn't wait to become a rich and famous NFL quarterback before starting his charity work. While he was still a student, Tebow would often spend his summer vacations and breaks on mission trips around the world, tending to the poor and spreading his faith.

With other University of Florida students, Tebow also helped raise money for the children's unit in a Florida hospital, for an orphanage in the Philippines, and to send disadvantaged children to Disney World.

When he graduated, he started the Tim Tebow Foundation. Early in 2012, the foundation, along with a charity known as CURE International, started construction on a children's hospital in the Philippines.

Sports writers around the country love to write about Tim Tebow, good and bad. His critics say he will never be a good starting NFL quarterback.

Tebow, who relies on his strong Christian faith, continues to make a name for himself in the NFL. But he knows there are more important things than football.

"I don't know what the future holds, but I know [God] holds my future," Tebow told ESPN Radio in March 2012. "That is something that has always given me peace and comfort. That's why I don't have to worry about the future. I can just worry about today and worry about becoming better as a football player and a person."

CHRONOLOGY

1987   Tim Tebow is born August 14.

2005   Is Florida's High School Player of the Year, starring for Nease High School.

2006   Plays in all 14 games as a college freshman for the national championship Florida Gators.

2007   Named starting quarterback for the Gators; December 8, is the first underclassman ever to win the prestigious Heisman Trophy.

2008   Named captain of the Florida Gators football team.

2009   Named offensive MVP as he leads the Gators to the national championship against Oklahoma.

2010   Drafted in the first round by the Denver Broncos; scores his first NFL touchdown.

2011   In October, replaces Kyle Orton as starting quarterback for the Broncos and defeats the Dolphins 18-15; announces plans to build children's hospital in the Philippines.

2012   Leads the Broncos to an improbable playoff victory against the Pittsburgh Steelers in January; in March, opens "Timmy's Playroom" for children suffering from terminal diseases; traded to the New York Jets.

Tim gets a hug from the Jacksonville Jaguars mascot.

NFL Stats

Year	Team	G	Att	Comp	Pct	Att/G	Yds	Avg	Yds/G	TD	Int	Rate
2011	Denver	14	271	126	46.5	19.4	1,729	6.4	123.5	12	6	72.9
2010	Denver	9	82	41	50.0	9.1	654	8.0	72.7	5	3	82.1
	TOTAL	23	353	167	47.3	15.3	2,383	6.8	103.6	17	9	75.1

College Stats

Year	School	Conf	Class	Pos	Cmp	Att	Pct	Yds	Y/A	TD	Int	Rate
2009	Florida	SEC	SR	QB	213	314	67.8	2895	9.2	21	5	164.2
2008	Florida	SEC	JR	QB	192	298	64.4	2746	9.2	30	4	172.4
2007	Florida	SEC	SO	QB	234	350	66.9	3286	9.4	32	6	172.5
2006	Florida	SEC	FR	QB	22	33	66.7	358	10.8	5	1	201.7
Career	Florida				661	995	66.4	9285	9.3	88	16	170.8

Tim addresses the New York media after his trade to the Jets.

Shipnuck, Alan. "Tim Tebow's Wild Ride." *Sports Illustrated,*
November 28, 2011. http://sportsillustrated.cnn.com/vault/
article/magazine/MAG1192439/index.htm

Tebow, Tim, and Nathan Whitaker. *Through My Eyes: A Quarterback's
Journey, Young Reader's Edition.* Grand Rapids, Michigan:
Zondervan Books, 2011.

Trotter, Jim. "4 Denver Broncos." *Sports Illustrated,* January 9, 2012.
http://sportsillustrated.cnn.com/vault/article/magazine/
MAG1193439/index.htm

Trotter, Jim. "The Power of the Possible." *Sports Illustrated,* December
19, 2011. http://sportsillustrated.cnn.com/vault/article/
magazine/MAG1193027/index.htm

Works Consulted

"2009 SEC Football Media Guide." SEC, 2009.

Battista, Judy. "Bradford Is No. 1, and Tebow Is Draft's Surprise." *The
New York Times,* April 23, 2010. http://www.nytimes.
com/2010/04/23/sports/football/23draft.html

Benbow, Julian. "In short time, Tebow has come a long way." *The
Boston Globe,* December 15, 2011. http://articles.boston.com/2011-
12-15/sports/30521248_1_tim-tebow-kyle-orton-mile-high-
messiah

Bob Tebow Evangelistic Association: "Tebow Family."
http://www.btea.org/aboutus.asp

Costello, Brian. "Tebow 'not sure' if he'll ever start for Jets." *New York
Post,* March 30, 2012.

Cravey, Beth Reese. "Tim Tebow returns to Jacksonville to open first of
his playrooms for ill children." *The Jacksonville Times-Union,* March
16, 2012. http://mayportmirror.jacksonville.com/news/health-
and-fitness/2012-03-15/story/tim-tebow-returns-jacksonville-
open-first-his-playrooms-ill

Kiszla, Mark. "Tebow saves job, then game." *The Denver Post,* January
9, 2012. http://www.post-gazette.com/stories/sports/steelers/
tebow-saves-job-then-game-216755/

Paige, Woody. "By Josh, Broncos got it right in draft." *The Denver Post,* April 23, 2010. http://www.deseretnews.com/article/700026874/By-Josh-Broncos-got-it-right-in-draft.html

Parler, Denver, ed. "Gator Football 2009 Media Guide." University of Florida, 2009.

Shipnuck, Alan. "Tim Tebow's Wild Ride." *Sports Illustrated,* November 28, 2011. http://sportsillustrated.cnn.com/vault/article/magazine/MAG1192439/index.htm

Tebow, Tim. Personal interview. October 23, 2011.

Tim Tebow: The Chosen One: An ESPN Original Documentary. ESPN, December 14, 2005. Television.

Trotter, Jim. "4 Denver Broncos." *Sports Illustrated,* January 9, 2012.

Trotter, Jim. "The Power of the Possible." *Sports Illustrated,* December 19, 2011. http://sportsillustrated.cnn.com/vault/article/magazine/MAG1193027/index.htm

Zinser, Lynn. "Tebow's Draft Magic." *The New York Times,* April 23, 2010. http://www.nytimes.com/2010/04/24/sports/24leadingoff.html

On the Internet
Bob Tebow Evangelistic Association: "Tebow Family"
http://www.btea.org/aboutus.asp

Florida Gators: "Tim Tebow"
http://www.gatorzone.com/football/misc.php?p=tebow/bio

The Official Website of Tim Tebow
http://www.timtebow.com

The Tim Tebow Foundation
http://www.timtebowfoundation.org

INDEX